LEGENDS OF WARFARE
GROUND

Ferdinand/Elefant
Panzerjäger Tiger (P)

DAVID DOYLE

SCHIFFER MILITARY

4880 Lower Valley Road   Atglen, PA 19310

Designed by Justin Watkinson
Type set in Impact/Minion Pro/Univers LT Std

ISBN: 978-0-7643-6643-7
Printed in India

Published by Schiffer Publishing, Ltd.
4880 Lower Valley Road
Atglen, PA 19310
Phone: (610) 593-1777; Fax: (610) 593-2002
Email: Info@schifferbooks.com
Web: www.schifferbooks.com

For our complete selection of fine books on this and related subjects, please visit our website at www.schifferbooks.com. You may also write for a free catalog.

Schiffer Publishing's titles are available at special discounts for bulk purchases for sales promotions or premiums. Special editions, including personalized covers, corporate imprints, and excerpts, can be created in large quantities for special needs. For more information, contact the publisher.

We are always looking for people to write books on new and related subjects. If you have an idea for a book, please contact us at proposals@schifferbooks.com.

Acknowledgments

This book would not have possible without the generous assistance of Thomas Anderson, David Fletcher, Massimo Foti, Tom Laemlein, the former staff of the Patton Museum, Tom Kailbourn, Scott Taylor, and Vladimir Yakubov. I have been especially honored to have the ongoing support of my wonderful wife, Denise, through this and my other projects.

Contents

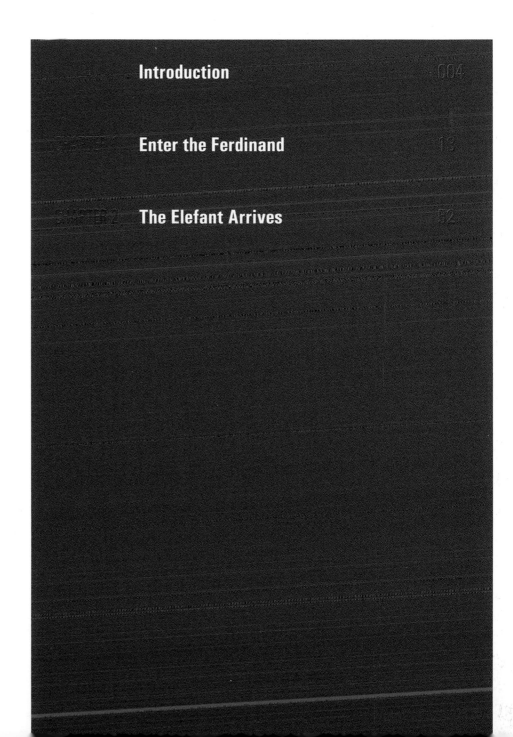

Introduction

The history of the Ferdinand, later called Elefant, begins with the famed Tiger program, and the fertile mind of automotive designer and engineer Dr. Ferdinand Porsche.

During 1939, his firm began work on a new German tank (then titled "Leopard"). Because Dr. Porsche was firmly convinced that a conventional power train would not hold up under the extreme weight of a heavy tank, he devised a new system. The Porsche Type 100, also known as the VK 3001 (P), used an innovative gas-electric drivetrain. Two large, air-cooled V-10 gasoline engines drove the generators, which in turn powered electric motors that acted as the final drives.

This concept was not as radical as it might sound, since the same propulsion method was (and still is) commonly used in railroad locomotives. After a wooden mockup was completed, three trial vehicles were ordered. However, only one unarmed trial vehicle was finished. In May 1941, Adolf Hitler ordered that the new tank's frontal armor be increased to 100 mm. Meanwhile, the 8.8 cm armament proposed for the VK 3001 (P) was retained, but the Führer desired increased armor penetration.

The redesigned tank was designated VK 4501 (P) by the army, and Type 101 by Porsche. In June 1942, it was redesignated Panzerkampfwagen VI Tiger. The displacement of the twin V-10 air-cooled engines was increased from 10 to 15 liters, and much of the Type 101 consisted of reworked or modified Type 100 components. Notably this included the unusual longitudinal torsion bar suspension, and the basic turret design. This turret, designed by Krupp, was also used on the Henschel-designed Tiger.

By August 1941, the project was included under the auspices of the "Tigerprogramm," and an all-out effort to complete the prototypes was well under way, with one hundred vehicles on the initial order. After defects in the newly designed engines (made by Simmering) caused some delays, a trial vehicle was delivered to Hitler's East Prussian headquarters in Rastenburg for a head-to-head competition with the Henschel vehicle. Hitler viewed the vehicle, and delivery took place as part of Hitler's birthday celebration on April 20, 1942.

During testing, the engines continued to cause problems, highlighted by excessive oil consumption and a short service life. Breakdowns were frequent, with the vehicle regularly becoming mired in soft earth. Ultimately, only a few of the one hundred Porsche Tigers were completed. Although most were used for training and testing purposes, they represented a sizable investment, in finances as well as resources—considerable amounts of raw materials, engineering design time, and labor man-hours had been devoted to the aborted Porsche-designed, gas-electric-powered Tiger (P) project. These all were resources the Germany could simply not afford to merely discard. Three of the hulls and chassis were repowered with liquid-cooled Maybach HL120 engines, replacing the troublesome Simmering-built Porsche air-cooled engines. These chassis were further modified and became "Berge-Panzer VI" recovery vehicles. In September 1942 it was decided to make use of the remaining chassis, and a significant portion of the Tiger (P) vehicles were modified into a self-propelled gun armed with an 8.8 cm Pak L/71 cannon.

The VK4501(P), also called the Tiger (P), was Porsche's reply to a July 1941 army requirement for a new heavy tank that would come to be known as the Tiger I. The vehicle featured a complicated propulsion system: two gasoline engines powered a pair of generators, which in turn powered two electric-drive motors that propelled the tracks. A Krupp-built turret contained an 88 mm KwK36 L/56 gun. Although a hundred examples were ordered, problems were encountered with the propulsion and suspension systems during development, and only ten vehicles were completed, with Henschel winning the contract to produce the Tiger tank. Shown here is one of the two test models of the Tiger (P) during trials at Döllersheim in August 1942. *Patton Museum*

Technicians and supervisors swarm over a VK4501(P), designated the Type 101 by Porsche, under construction at the firm's Nibelungenwerke in Sankt-Valentin, Austria, with several unfinished chassis in the background. The angled hull plate with the vision slit to the side of the machine gun mount in the front of the vehicle was a feature that would carry over to the Ferdinand/Elefant tank destroyers. *Patton Museum*

The turret has yet to be installed on the same VK4501(P), which was the first example of the *Fahrgestell* (chassis) Type 101. On the Tiger (P), the twin engines and generators were located toward the rear of the hull, as were the electric-drive motors and the sprockets. *Patton Museum*

The headlights of the Tiger (P) were mounted on the fenders; by contrast, the headlights of the Ferdinand/Elefant were attached to the hull. In the background is the full-sized wooden mockup of Type 100, Tiger (P). *Patton Museum*

This series of photos of workers swarming over the Tiger (P) Type 101 was staged for propaganda purposes, to illustrate the extraordinary measures Porsche took to finish the chassis so that it could be driven in an official demonstration on Hitler's birthday, on April 20, 1942. *Patton Museum*

A Tiger (P) chassis undergoes tests of the vehicle's ability to operate in dusty conditions. In the absence of an actual turret, a concrete cylinder has been installed over the turret's opening to replicate its weight. The vehicle ran on Kgs 62/600/130 tracks, which were 600 mm (23.62 inches) wide and had a pitch of 130 mm (5.12 inches). *Patton Museum*

The same Tiger (P) stirs up dust on the test range. The ball mount for the bow machine gun (minus the machine gun) and the driver's vision port and cover were similar to those elements as they would appear on the Henschel Tiger I tank. The "turret" had a roof with a hatch and two forward-vision openings. *Patton Museum*

During the dust tests, the Tiger (P) chassis was modified with covers over the air intake grilles on the sides of the hull and two boxes containing air filters on a redesigned engine compartment cover between the air intakes. These covers and filters were not installed on the few production Tiger (P)s. *Patton Museum*

Dr. Ferdinand Porsche (*in the dark fedora*) was photographed at Nibelungenwerke in August 1942. Dr. Porsche was a favorite of Hitler's, and the Führer was upset when Porsche's entry failed to win the Tiger tank competition. In the background is a Tiger (P) with a Krupp turret. There are narrow (23.62 inches wide) fenders at the front and rear of the vehicle, and no fender along the sponson of the hull. Later Tiger (P)s would have front and rear fenders that were 27.56 inches wide and sponson fenders 7.87 inches wide. There is a radio antenna mount toward the rear of the hull, to the rear of the right air intake. *Patton Museum*

This vehicle is one of two Tiger (P)s undergoing tests at Döllersheim, Germany, in August 1942. These two vehicles were fitted with Krupp turrets no. 4 and 8. The narrow fenders were mounted on this tank. On the upper rear of the turret, which is traversed to the rear, are six brackets for stowing spare track links. *Patton Museum*

Technicians confer on the rear deck of a Tiger (P) during tests at Döllersheim. The turret was the same model that would be used on the early-production Henschel Tiger I, Type E. Pulled over the muzzle of the 88 mm KwK 46 L/56 gun is a canvas cover. *Patton Museum*

A Tiger (P) sits in thick mud during tests. The vertical plate in front of the driver's and bow gunner's compartment was 100 mm thick, while the angled plates to the side of that plate were 80 mm thick. The vision slits incorporated into disks on those angled plates were similar to the vision slit toward the front of the side of the turret. *Patton Museum*

Technicians and officials at Döllersheim check over the engines of a Tiger (P). Large towing eyes were welded to an otherwise uncluttered plate, 80 mm thick, at the rear of the hull. A standard vehicular jack is lying on the rear deck above the air grille. *Patton Museum*

Several Tiger (P)s were detailed as troop-training tanks to schwere Panzer-Abteilung 503 at Döllersheim. The one in the foreground, equipped with *Turm* (turret) no. 7 and a Pz.Kpfw. IV-type stowage box on the rear of the turret, got stuck while trying to cross a ditch, and two other Tiger (P)s are about to recover the vehicle. *Patton Museum*

Panzerjäger Tiger (P)	Specifications
Length	8.14 meters
Width	3.38 meters
Height	2.97 meters
Weight (Ferdinand)	65 tons
Weight (Elefant)	70 tons
Fuel capacity	950 liters
Maximum speed	30 km/hr.
Range, on road	150 kilometers
Range, cross-country	90 kilometers
Crew	6
Communications Fu 5 and Fu 2, intercom	
Weapon, main	8.8 cm Pak 43/2 L/71
Weapon, secondary (Elefant)	7.92 mm MG 34
Ammunition stowage, main	50 rounds

Panzerjäger Tiger (P)	Specifications
Ammunition stowage, secondary	600 rounds
Engine make	2 × Maybach
Engine model	HL 120 TRM
Engine configuration	V-12, liquid cooled
Engine displacement	11.9 liters
Engine horsepower	265 @ 2,600 rpm

* All measurements are given in the metric system.

CHAPTER 1
Enter the Ferdinand

The new Tiger (P)–based Sturmgeschütz would feature two prominent elements—very heavy armor protection and an extremely potent antitank gun, the 8.8 cm Pak L/71 cannon. This weapon was installed in a boxlike superstructure, with frontal armor measuring a whopping 200 mm thick. These vehicles were repowered in a manner like that used with the Bergepanzer VI, using Maybach HL120 liquid-cooled engines to turn the generators, which powered the electric traction motors driving the tracks. The huge, new tank hunter is often referred to as the Panzerjäger "Tiger P." However, in February 1943, it was officially dubbed "Ferdinand" in honor of Dr. Ferdinand Porsche.

The now-surplus ninety unused turrets and 88 mm guns were adapted for use on Henschel Tigers. The Altmärkische Kettenfabrik GmbH, abbreviated to "Alkett," completed the design work on the new heavy Panzerjäger in November 1942. Two of the one hundred hulls, which had been completed by Krupp and shipped to Nibelungenwerk prior to the suspension of the Tiger (P) program, were sent to Alkett. Alkett used these to complete two trial vehicles (chassis numbers 150010 and 15011).

Originally, Alkett was to produce all the superstructures while Nibelungenwerk would complete the chassis. This plan was revised in February 1943, due to concerns that the project would interfere with Alkett's Sturmgeschütz (StuG) III production. Eisenwerk Oberdonau, in Linz, was then assigned to assemble the chassis, while Krupp, in Eisen, would make the superstructure, and Nibelungenwerk, at St. Valentin, would handle the final assembly. Nibelungenwerk took only two months to roll out eighty-nine Ferdinands, chassis numbers 150012 through 150100, beginning production in April 1943 and finishing by May 8.

The massive new tank killers were dispatched to the Russian Front the next month, as part of Panzerjäger-Abteilung 656. The vehicles' first combat came during Operation Zitadelle, the massive tank battles at Kursk, beginning on July 5, 1943. By December, combat losses and breakdowns had reduced their number to forty-eight, all of which were returned to Nibelungenwerk to be rebuilt.

The two Alkett-produced prototypes of the Ferdinand underwent initial testing at the Kummersdorf proving ground beginning on April 12, 1943. As a result of these tests, Krupp fabricated an armored collar to be mounted on the gun tube. This was intended to keep shell splatter, fragments, and small-arms fire from entering the fighting compartment via gaps in the gun mount. Since Ferdinand production was well underway by that time, the shields were intended to be installed in the field. Unfortunately, adequate supplies failed to reach the combat units in time, and many Ferdinands entered combat without the shields.

The Ferdinand tank destroyers were assigned to schwere Panzerjäger-Abteilung 653 and 654. Each of these Panzerjäger battalions consisted of three companies, with each company divided into three platoons. Vehicles were assigned in this fashion:

- Each platoon included four Ferdinands.
- Each company headquarters had two Ferdinands.
- Battalion headquarters had three Ferdinands.
- Each schwere Panzerjäger-Abteilung had a total of forty-five Ferdinands.

Both battalions were part of the schwere Panzerjäger-Regiment 656 and were committed to Operation Citadel. When the attack began on July 5, 1943, the heavy tank destroyers had considerable success, advancing as far as Aleksandrovka and destroying twenty-six Soviet T-34s along the way. However, this success came at a high cost, with thirty-three of the forty-five vehicles damaged, primarily due to mines. Several of the damaged Ferdinands were recovered, repaired, and returned to action. From the onset of Operation Citadel until August 7, 1943, the 653rd lost thirteen Ferdinands, but their 88 mm guns were credited with destroying 320 Soviet tanks.

Meanwhile, the Schwere Panzerjäger-Abteilung 654 advanced toward Ol'khovatka, losing eighteen of its vehicles to various causes, and were unable to recover any of those put out of action. On July 14, a small force of Ferdinands under the command of Lt. Henrich Teriete were deployed as part of a relief force to rescue the 36th Infantry Regiment, which was surrounded by Soviet forces. The heavy tank destroyers performed admirably, wiping out large numbers of Soviet tanks, with Lt. Henrich Teriete's vehicle accounting for twenty-two Soviet tanks by itself.

Initial actions showed that the Ferdinand had amazing antitank capability, but that it could also be immobilized by land mines and then destroyed by roving Soviet infantry antitank teams. Since the Ferdinand did not have machine guns for local defense of the vehicle, Russian tank hunters were able to overwhelm the crew of a disabled Ferdinand rather easily. Desperate times call for desperate measures, and in one situation the crew of the Ferdinand commanded by Karl-Heinz Noak opened the breech of their 88 mm gun and fired an MG 34 machine gun through the bore at attacking infantry. Soon after, the 654 Abteilung's maintenance company created several expedient machine gun mounts, using spent 88 mm shell casings, which permitted an MG 34 or MG 42 to be fitted in the cannon breech. The machine gun was then aimed by using the main gun's elevation and traverse controls. Though crude, this proved a better solution than fitting platforms to the rear of the vehicles so that infantry could ride the Ferdinand into battle. Troops in these exposed positions suffered heavy casualties.

Another weakness of the Ferdinand design was found in the engine compartment and cooling system, which proved vulnerable to shell fragments, plunging fire from mortars and artillery, and Molotov cocktails used by Soviet tank-hunter units. During August 1943, the 654th transferred its remaining Ferdinand tank destroyers to the 653rd. On December 10, 1943, schwere Panzerjäger-Regiment 656, including schwere Panzerjäger-Abteilung 653, was relieved and ordered to Sankt-Polten, as the weary Ferdinand returned to the Reich for some needed rest, overhaul, and modernization.

The first two *Ferdinands, Fahrgestell Nummer* (chassis number / Fgst. Nr.) 150010 and 150011, were test vehicles at Kummersdorff through December 1943. The round plate on the hull was a filled-in hatch that had been present on the Tiger (P). The first Ferdinands lacked reinforcing plates at the lower front of the superstructure.

VK.4501 (P)

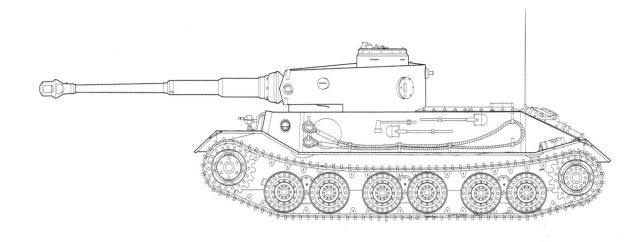

Elefant

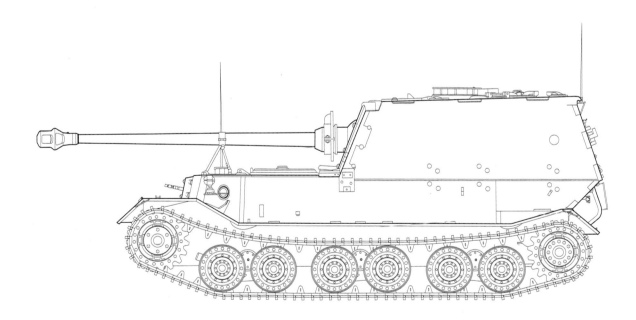

The first several Ferdinands were issued with protective guards for the headlight mounts; these were soon discontinued. A jack stored on the glacis was later moved to the rear of the hull. Two of the conical-headed bolts that were situated on the lower right-hand side of the plate at the front of the hull are missing.

Ferdinand Fgst. Nr. 150054 and tactical number 501 was the vehicle of the commander of the 1st Platoon, 1st Company, schwere Panzerjäger-Abteilung 654. Captured in the Battle of Kursk, the vehicle now resides at the Kubinka Tank Museum near Moscow, Russia.

The letter *N* on the left mud flap of Ferdinand number 501 stood for Hauptmann Karl-Heinz Noak, the commander of the battalion. The right mud flap is missing, and the lenses of the Bosch headlights have been broken out. Large clevises are installed on the towing eyes. *The Tank Museum*

Ferdinand Armor	Protection
Superstructure front	200 mm
Superstructure side	80 mm
Superstructure rear	80 mm
Superstructure roof	30 mm
Hull front	100 mm + 100 mm
Hull lower front	80 mm
Hull side	80 mm
Hull rear	80 mm
Driver's compartment front	100 mm + 100 mm
Engine deck	80 mm
Forward bottom	30 mm + 20 mm
Rear bottom	80 mm

Ferdinand chassis number 150080 of schwere Panzerjäger-Abteilung 653, tactical number 121, in a Soviet town before the Battle of Kursk, shows that it bore a tactical sign on the rear of the superstructure that is barely visible in the preceding photo due to glare. The small hollow square over the solid white square with diagonal red line stood for 3rd Platoon, 1st Company. *Thomas Anderson collection*

The black-outlined tactical number, 121, is barely visible at the center of the right side of the superstructure in another view of the previous vehicle. The two lower ladder rungs on the left rear of the superstructure have been removed. *Thomas Anderson collection*

Three Ferdinands of schwere Panzerjäger-Abteilung 653 sit along a Soviet city street in the days before the launching of Operation Citadel: the Battle of Kursk. The tow cable of the first vehicle is severely tangled, a breach of proper precautions since it was imperative to keep tow cables in tip-top condition at all times. *Thomas Anderson collection*

At the Battle of Kursk, schwere Panzerjäger-Regiment 656, the parent unit of schwere Panzerjäger-Abteilung 653 and 654, included a number of PzKpfw IIIs in Headquarters Company. It is likely that one of those headquarters tanks was the one photographed next to an unidentified Ferdinand. *Thomas Anderson collection*

A crewman kneels on the roof of the superstructure of the number 534 Ferdinand while another man lies on the roof. The dark object on the deck is the left engine access cover. Though missing its front right fender, the vehicle survived the battalion's battles in July and August 1943. *Thomas Anderson collection*

This vehicle was assigned to schwere Panzerjäger-Abteilung 653 during the July 1943 offensive at Kursk.

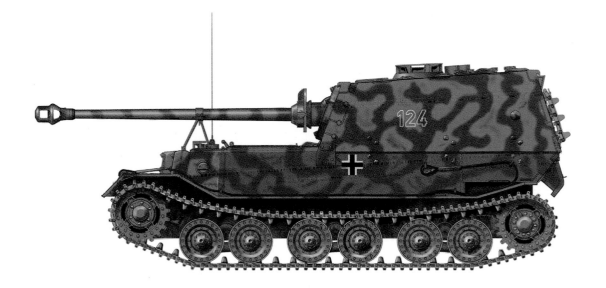

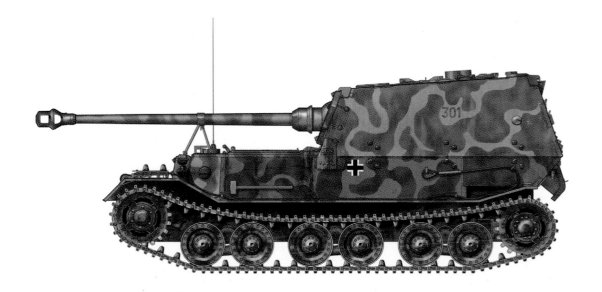

Camouflaged with large patches of dark green over the *Dunkelgelb* base coat, 301 was commanded by Oblt. Salamon on the first day of the Kursk battle. The vehicle was assigned to 3rd Company, I/656 schwere Panzerjäger-Regiment.

Ferdinand number 501 of schwere Panzerjäger-Abteilung 654 was damaged by a mine in the Battle of Kursk and captured by the Soviets. The tool box on the side is open, and only the two tow hooks remain in place. This vehicle is preserved at the Kubinka Tank Museum in Russia. *The Tank Museum*

A Soviet photographer captured a view of number 501 disabled in the minefield. After the tank hunter struck a mine, its crew tried to destroy the vehicle by detonating an explosive charge inside the fighting compartment. However, the vehicle survived in sufficiently intact condition for the Soviets to claim it as a war trophy. *The Tank Museum*

Ferdinand number 501 of schwere Panzerjäger-Abteilung 654 suffered what appears to have been a nonpenetrating hit from a shell to the rear of the tactical number on the superstructure. The splash marks from this damage are still visible on the vehicle at Kubinka. This photo was taken after the Soviets had made some rudimentary repairs to the suspension. *The Tank Museum*

The number 501 Ferdinand lies on the Kursk battlefield. Splash marks from a projectile that evidently failed to penetrate the side of the superstructure are to the rear of the remnants of the tactical number. The driver's hatch door is open, exposing the top of the periscope housing to view. *Thomas Anderson collection*

This cross-sectional view shows the general arrangement of the interior of the Ferdinand. At center is the Maybach engine, coupled to the generator just forward of it. At the lower rear of the lower hull is the traction motor, and above that, ammunition stowage. At the very front of the hull is the driver's position.

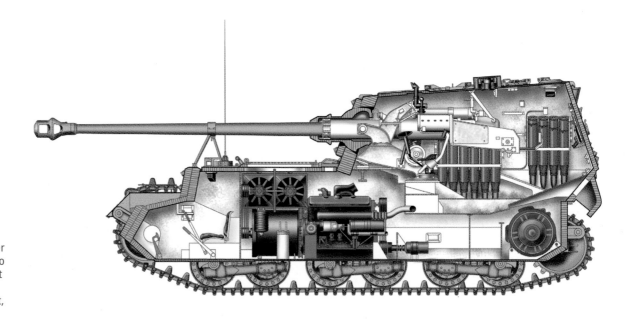

The Soviets considered their capture of several Ferdinands at Kursk an intelligence coup. Here, Red Army personnel inspect two of the vehicles, from schwere Panzerjäger-Abteilung 654, on the battleground: tactical number 702 in the foreground and 723 behind. Damage to 702 included the loss of the 88 mm gun muzzle and brake. *Thomas Anderson collection*

Ferdinand tactical number 624, chassis number (Fgst. Nr.) 150090, was a much-photographed war trophy of the Soviets. The vehicle was assigned to the 2nd Company, schwere Panzerjäger-Abteilung 654, at the time of the Battle of Kursk in the summer of 1943. The Ferdinand was disabled in the vicinity of Orël when it ran over a mine, which severed a track, and the crew abandoned the vehicle on the field. Subsequently, the Soviets took great pains to photograph the Ferdinand where it lay on the battlefield, both for propaganda and intelligence-gathering purposes. It is not clear if the evident marking immediately to the rear of the national cross was an insignia or had other significance. Subsequent to photographing Ferdinand tactical number 624, the Soviets repaired the tracks and transported the vehicle to Moscow, where it was displayed to the public as an example of the Red Army's ability to overcome German armor, even a vehicle as massive and heavily armed and armored as the Ferdinand. Although the photographs of disabled and destroyed Ferdinands presented here portray the physical effects of Soviet mines and antitank fire, these images do not entirely convey the chaos and terror of armored combat at Kursk. In a magazine article published in the years after World War II, former *Unteroffizier* Heinz Leuschen, who had been present at the battle as a member of schwere Panzerjäger-Abteilung 654, recounted an attack that took place on July 5, 1943. Initially his crew's morale was high, and they were singing as they proceeded into battle under fire from Soviet antitank batteries. Soon, however, a tank escorting the Ferdinands struck a mine and was disabled. Shortly thereafter, Leuschen's Ferdinand detonated an antitank mine. He described the shock, confusion, and painful sensations that ensued. The crew quickly regained their composure and set about assessing damage to their vehicle. The track had been severed and a few of the road wheels were destroyed. The crew had just begun to perform repairs during a lull in the firing when a Soviet artillery round exploded nearby, killing two of the crewmen. Leuschen and the vehicle commander climbed back inside the Ferdinand, while the other two surviving crewmen set out to get help. Soviet forces continued to try to knock out the tank with artillery fire but failed to score a direct hit. Late that afternoon, the German maintenance section was able to rescue Leuschen and his commander. *Thomas Anderson collection*

The Soviets took this view of the left side of the Ferdinand with tactical number 624 of the 2nd Company, schwere Panzerjäger-Abteilung 654, following its capture at Kursk. The number 26 on the hull evidently was applied by the Soviets. An informational placard is propped up on the front of the right track while on display at Gor'ky Park, Moscow, in mid-1944. *Patton Museum*

While on display during World War II, Ferdinand 624 was photographed close-up, showing the Russian informational placard. In front of the superstructure, the right engine compartment access door is partially open. The long tube secured to the fender was a storage container for the radio antenna. *The Tank Museum*

The left front fender of Ferdinand number 624 was crumpled. Several spare track links were still stored on the glacis. With the hatch doors open, the mounts for the driver's three periscopes are visible. The travel lock is disengaged from the 88 mm gun and is folded forward. *The Tank Museum*

Visible on the driver's and radio operator's hatch doors of Ferdinand number 624 are the locking handles (note their different locations) and the links to the coil springs inside the hatches, which acted as assists in opening the heavy doors. A clear view is offered of the Kgs 62/600/130 tracks. *The Tank Museum*

After its capture, Ferdinand number 624 is on display in the Soviet Union along with other German military vehicles. An informational placard in Russian is on the fender. With the rear hatch cover removed, the thickness of the rear wall of the superstructure can be gauged. The pistol port plug on the left side is missing. *The Tank Museum*

The gun shield comprised two armored plates clamped over the mantlet. At first the shields were installed with the bolts and nuts facing toward the rear, but this made it difficult to access those fasteners. As a field fix, some Ferdinand crews reversed the shield, as shown here, and this configuration became standard with the Elefant. *The Tank Museum*

Ferdinand number 624 had been assigned to the 3rd Platoon, 2nd Company, of schwere Panzerjäger-Abteilung 654. It was disabled by a mine at Kursk, which led to its capture by the Soviets. The missing road wheel, as evident here, is likely attributable to the mine damage. The vehicle features sprayed-on green camouflage. *The Tank Museum*

The right side of number 624 Ferdinand is shown in another photograph taken at a Soviet captured-armor display. The gun shield is in its original configuration, with the bolt flanges and reinforcing ribs facing toward the rear and the flat surface facing forward. The sprayed green camouflage paint was even applied to the radio antenna tube. *Military History Institute*

At least two large-caliber antitank rounds penetrated the left hull at the front of the engines/generators compartment of this Ferdinand captured by the Soviets. Another projectile hit the side plate of the driver's compartment, leaving splinter marks around the vision slit but apparently not penetrating the armor. The fender was sheared away. *The Tank Museum*

Another Soviet photo of a captured Ferdinand on the Kursk battlefield. This image was used by US intelligence for AFV identification training.

A Ferdinand rolls down a dirt road past a Maultier half-track truck and a motorcycle with sidecar. Sitting on top of the driver's compartment is a crewman. The vehicle has rain gutters on the front of the superstructure, and its mostly light-colored appearance is interrupted by what appear to be a few slightly darker camouflaged spots. *Thomas Anderson collection*

The hulk of a Ferdinand of schwere Panzerjäger-Abteilung 654 sits in a field near Kursk. The rear hatch cover, probably blown free by an internal explosion, lies on the ground next to the left track. The white letter N on the lower left rear of the superstructure signified Hauptmann Noak's battalion. *The Tank Museum*

Ferdinand tactical number 133 (chassis number 150019) of schwere Panzerjäger Abteilung 653 rolls down a road, with most of the crewmen sitting on the deck. The commander of the vehicle, Feldwebel Heinz Rempel, sits next to the driver, whose head is poking up through his hatch. *Thomas Anderson collection*

Several crewmen sit on a flatcar behind Ferdinand number 621 of the 3rd Platoon, 2nd Company, of schwere Panzerjäger-Abteilung 654. This vehicle, Fgst. Nr. 150068, was en route to Bryansk, USSR, for repairs after the Battle of Kursk. *Thomas Anderson collection*

A Ferdinand of the 3rd Company, schwere Panzerjäger-Abteilung 653, has been loaded onto a flatcar for shipment. A rough coat of whitewash has been applied to the vehicle as winter camouflage. The gun is safely cradled in the travel lock. *Thomas Anderson collection*

Two Ferdinands proceed abreast, churning up a significant amount of dust. The commander and a gun crewman of the vehicle in the foreground are standing in their hatches to better view their surroundings, and the driver has his hatch door open. A shrub has been stuck behind the tow cable to lend a measure of camouflage. *Thomas Anderson collection*

Four men from a Ferdinand crew pose casually in front of their vehicle. They are wearing a mix of headwear, including a black beret, possibly a souvenir from training in Rouen, France. The camouflage paint is very subtle, and foliage has been wrapped around the 88 mm gun barrel to break up its outline. *Thomas Anderson collection*

Seven Panzerjäger personnel are lined up next to number 513, a Ferdinand attached to the 2nd Platoon, 1st Company, schwere Panzerjäger-Abteilung 654. Close examination reveals that a very fine network of green paint was sprayed on the barrel, whereas larger patterns were applied to the hull and superstructure. *Thomas Anderson collection*

The seven crewmen have moved up onto the Ferdinand for another photograph. Now revealed, in addition to the missing front end of the right fender, is a badly bent section near the rear of the fender. The glare on the side of the superstructure has caused the white tactical number to fade into the *Dunkelgelb* paint. *Thomas Anderson collection*

In addition to the spare tracks fastened to the fenders on this Ferdinand of schwere Panzerjäger-Abteilung 653, three rows of track links are stowed on the glacis. A close inspection reveals that the gun shield had been turned around, with the flanges and fastening bolts and nuts facing forward. *Thomas Anderson collection*

In the USSR, an Sd.Kfz. 7 half-track towing an 88 mm gun passes a Ferdinand of the 4th Platoon, 3rd Company, schwere Panzerjäger-Abteilung 653. The vehicle had suffered a breakdown during the retreat from Nikopol', Ukraine, in early December 1943. The unit symbol is visible on the upper right of the rear of the superstructure. *Thomas Anderson collection*

Seen at what appears to be a forward base, this Ferdinand displays on the rear of its superstructure a tactical sign adopted by schwere Panzerjäger-Abteilung 653 before the Battle of Kursk. Depending on the color of the marking, it signified the 2nd Platoon of either the 1st Company (white) or 3rd Company (yellow). *Thomas Anderson collection*

Several crewmen of a Ferdinand of schwere Panzerjäger-Abteilung 653 take time to pose for a portrait while being briefed by a staff officer from their battalion's parent unit, schwere Panzerjäger-Regiment 656. This vehicle has sloped rain gutters on front of the superstructure, a field modification later standardized on the Elefant. *Thomas Anderson collection*

Conflicting information exists on the battalion and tactical numbers and cause of destruction of this Ferdinand that met its end at Kursk. The tool box has been emptied of its contents. *Thomas Anderson collection*

The 88 mm gun and its cradle have remained attached to the front plate of the superstructure of this wrecked Ferdinand, which is seen in profile. On the ground to the far right is the gun shield, with the gun barrel stuck through it. *Thomas Anderson collection*

Commanded by Unteroffizier Horst Golinski and assigned to the 1st Company of schwere Panzerjäger-Abteilung 653 during Unternehmen Zitadelle ("Operation Citadel"), Ferdinand number 132 was photographed by the Soviets on or about July 7, 1943, after its destruction in the vicinity of Ponyri in the Soviet 70th Army sector. A mine blast took off the two left front road wheels and the related suspension assembly and severed the track. Since the crew had no means of recovering the vehicle, they detonated charges inside it to render it unusable to the enemy. It is likely that it was the scuttling explosion that blew the deck above the engine compartment off its mountings, leaving it lying askew atop the hull. From the blackened condition of the 88 mm gun barrel and the front plate of the fighting compartment, it appears that a fire of considerable proportions broke out in the engine compartment when the crew scuttled the Ferdinand. There is also a blackened area on the side of the hull, partially obscuring the Balkenkreuz. A section of the severed track is lying on the ground toward the left. The light-colored object lying next to the track section is a towing clevis. Another one of these heavy-duty clevises is faintly visible on the ground just beyond the front right of the vehicle. One of the blown-off road wheels is lying in the foreground. The force of the explosion blew the left fender upward. The hinged panel to the front of the right fender is poised in the raised position. To the lower left of the front plate of the fighting compartment, the right access door with built-in ventilation scoop is in the open position. It is not clear if this door was blown open by the explosion or if the Soviets opened it while inspecting the vehicle. Toward the rear of the side of the fighting compartment, the pistol port plug has been unfastened from its position and is hanging from its chain. *Thomas Anderson collection*

Crewmen stand by near their Ferdinand parked in a farmyard. Tow cables are attached with clevises to the front towing eyes, ready to be put to use at a moment's notice should the vehicle become disabled. On the side of the hull is a sledgehammer, later moved to the rear of the superstructure. A jack and block are on the glacis. *Thomas Anderson collection*

A Ferdinand receives ammunition from a Büssing-NAG 4500 truck. Rain gutters have been fastened to the front of the superstructure, a feature that later would be standardized on the Elefant. The vehicle seems to have just a few splotches of dark paint on the side to interrupt the *Dunkelgelb* base color. *Thomas Anderson collection*

The tactical sign on the upper right rear of the superstructure, white with a diagonal red line, indicates that this Ferdinand was attached to the 3rd Platoon, 1st Company, schwere Panzerjäger-Abteilung 653. A stowage box has been mounted above the rear hatch of the superstructure, and a wooden crate is on the roof. *Thomas Anderson collection*

The commander surveys the terrain as an unidentified Ferdinand of schwere Panzerjäger-Abteilung 654 makes its way through an evergreen thicket. The distinctive crisscross camouflage of that battalion blended well with the foliage. *Thomas Anderson collection*

A crewman in a touring cap and overalls takes a cigarette break on Ferdinand 612 of the 2nd Platoon, 2nd Company, schwere Panzerjäger-Abteilung 654. Numerous details are visible, including the hold-open lock for the driver's hatch door, the sledgehammer bracket on the side of the hull, and spare track links lying on the left side of the glacis. This vehicle was under the command of Leutnant Heyn in Operation Citadel, following which it was transferred to schwere Panzerjäger-Abteilung 653. *Thomas Anderson collection*

A rare wartime photograph of both the Ferdinand driver's and radio operator's hatch doors open provides comparative details of the interiors of the doors. The latch handle of the radio operator's door was at the front corner, while the handle on the driver's door was on the side toward the vehicle's center because of the positioning of the periscopes. *Thomas Anderson collection*

A track-replacement job is underway on a Ferdinand. The left idler has been removed, revealing its bearing. The second man from left is leaning on a hammer, used for knocking out and driving in track pins. The absence of the fender, whether through battle damage or intentional removal, would have eased the task at hand. *Thomas Anderson collection*

Two crewmen pose in front of their Ferdinand number 513, wearing double-breasted panzer crew jackets and side caps (*Feldmützen*). With the two men providing scale, the relatively massive size of the towing clevises is evident. Lying loosely on top of the spare track sections is the tow cable. *Thomas Anderson collection*

Seven crewmen lounge on the number 513 Ferdinand, with another Ferdinand in the background pointing in the opposite direction. This vehicle was chassis number 150036 and belonged to schwere Panzerjäger-Abteilung 654. The front sections of the fenders are removed. *Thomas Anderson collection*

The 612 Ferdinand of schwere Panzerjäger-Abteilung 654, commanded by a Leutnant Heyn, displays its crisscross camouflage of green over Dunkelgelb. This scheme was also referred to as a "net" or "web" pattern. Note the jerry can on the front deck. *Thomas Anderson collection*

Ferdinand number 612 was photographed at a maintenance area near Karachev, USSR, in August 1943, around the time it and the other vehicles of the 654th were transferred to schwere Panzerjäger-Abteilung 653. The dark swatches of paint on the hull evidently indicate repaired areas. *Thomas Anderson collection*

Faintly visible on the superstructure of this Ferdinand is the tactical number 134 in black outline, signifying it is the fourth vehicle in the 4th Platoon, 1st Company, schwere Panzerjäger-Abteilung 653. Local camouflage has been draped over the hull. *Thomas Anderson collection*

Near the time of the Battle of the Dnieper, a Ferdinand parked alongside a road is passed by a column of German armored vehicles, including a second Elefant from schwere Panzerjäger-Abteilung 654. These vehicles have had their gun shields reversed to ease maintenance. *Tom Laemlein collection*

This photo of number 714 Ferdinand features a close-up study of the front end of the vehicle, including a clear view of the inside of the driver's hatch and periscopes and the Kgs 62/600/130 tracks. The jack rests on the glacis, and both tow cables are secured to clevises on the towing eyes for rapid deployment if necessary. *Thomas Anderson collection*

The number 714 Ferdinand (chassis number 150034654) served with schwere Panzerjäger-Abteilung 654. With the vehicle parked in the cover of woods, the crew relaxes, with the man holding the newspaper sitting wedged in between the gun shield and superstructure. The camouflage scheme is noteworthy for its subtlety. *Thomas Anderson collection*

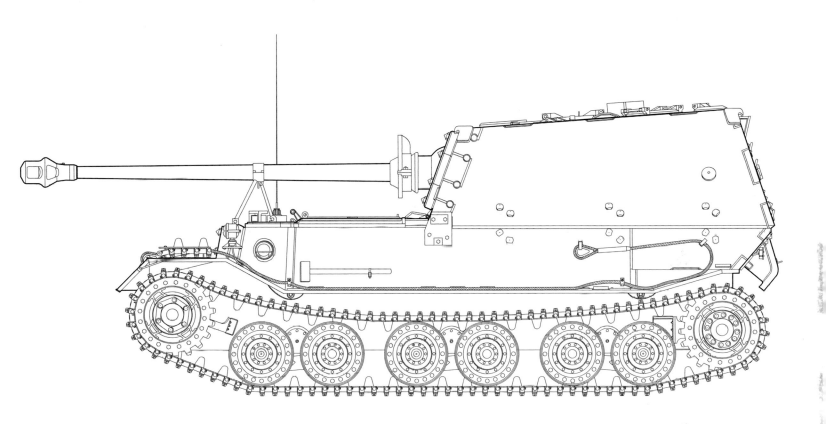

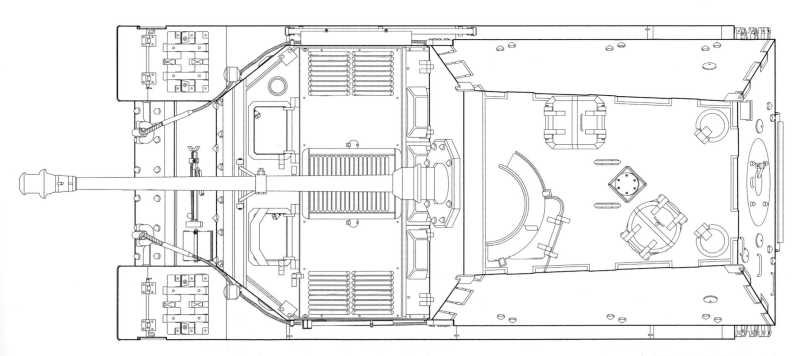

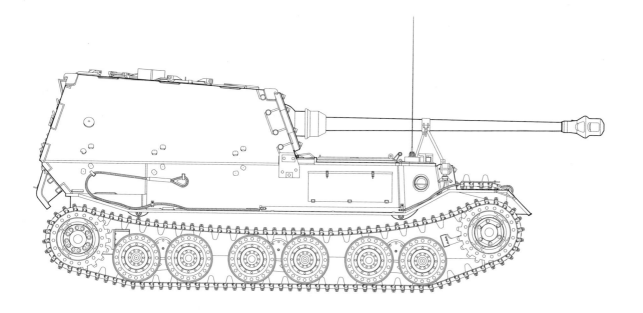

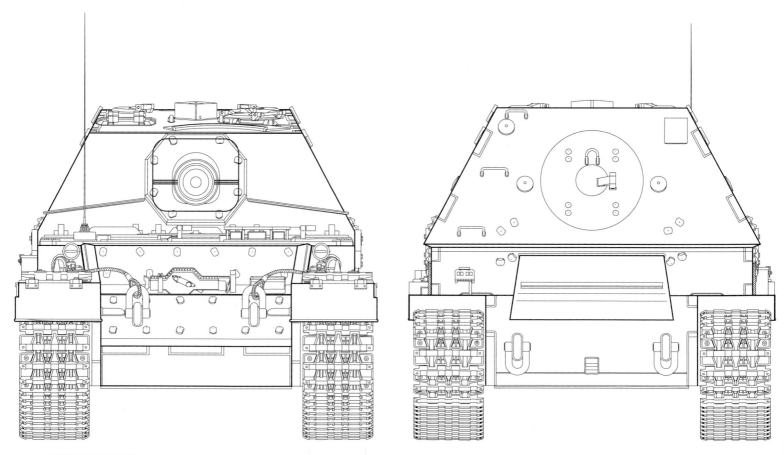

Preserved at the Kubinka Tank Museum in Russia's Moscow Region is the only surviving Ferdinand tank hunter. The vehicle, Fgst. Nr. 150072, assigned to schwere Panzerjäger-Abteilung 654, was disabled by a mine at the Battle of Kursk in July 1943 and captured by the Soviets.

The headlights on this Ferdinand are Soviet replacements, not the original Bosch units. The gun shield, however, is in its original configuration, with the bolts and flanges connecting the upper and lower parts facing to the rear. Toward the front of the side of the hull are four tapped holes, to which the toolbox, missing on this example, would have been bolted.

The road wheels had steel tires, each of which was cushioned with a rubber ring housed within the wheel. The wheels were mounted in pairs on torsion-bar casings, which in turn were attached to rocker arms that pivoted on bearings mounted to the hull. The front-mounted idlers had sprockets to improve vehicular handling and regulate the slack of the upper track.

On the Kubinka Ferdinand, a triangular piece of sheet metal covers the recess between the fender and the hull above the rearmost road wheel. It is not clear whether this was a German modification or an addition by the Soviets after they captured the vehicle. At the lower front corner of the superstructure is a reinforcing plate, also bolted to the hull.

At the rear of the Ferdinand is the right drive sprocket, 36.22 inches in diameter and with nineteen teeth on each rim. It is mounted to its bearing with twelve lug nuts. The fenders are of diamond-tread plate. Conical-headed bolts secure the superstructure (sometimes called the gun box) to the hull. A pistol port is toward the rear of the side of the superstructure.

The superstructure of the Ferdinand was of welded construction, with all joints being interleaved, or finger-jointed, with the exception of the one between the vertical front plate and the roof. The side plates were 80 mm thick, while the rear plate was 80 mm. The rear joints of the hull were also finger-jointed.

The shroud protruding from the rear of the hull is a cooling-air intake for the two Siemens type 1495A electric motors that powered the drive sprockets. The air intake is on the underside of the housing. At the upper right of the rear plate of the superstructure is the mount for an antenna when a command radio was installed.

The hot-air exhaust shroud for the electric motors is protected by a steel screen. Plugs with holes to accept the tow shackles were welded into the U-shaped towing eyes. Between the towing eyes is a towing pintle, the upper fork of which has been flattened. The bracket to the right of the left towing eye may be the remnant of a jack bracket.

On the rear of the superstructure of the Ferdinand was a circular hatch with a removable cover. This cover is a blank replacement that was tack-welded in place; the original one had eight large, conical bolt heads on the exterior surface, along with a spent-shell ejector port and a lifting lug above the ejector port.

Above the mud flap on the left side of the rear of the hull is the mounting bracket for the blackout taillight, above which is a guard for the light. The two vertical rods welded to the superstructure above that guard are all that remains of the lowest of the three steel ladder rungs that provided crewmen a means of climbing to the roof.

The left side of the Ferdinand at Kubinka lacks the sheet-metal cover over the triangular recess between the fender and the hull. Mounted on the side of the hull are clamps and brackets for a tow cable. The welded joints of the hull and superstructure are visible in close-up.

The vertical face of the hull in front of the driver's and radio operator's compartment and the upper vertical plate at the front of the hull were fabricated from two 100 mm thick armor plates placed one on top of the other and fastened together with conical-headed bolts. The frontal plate of the superstructure was a single 200 mm plate. *Vladimir Yakubov*

On the roof are, *left to right*, the gunner's periscope aperture and its covers; commander's hatch (*opposite side of roof*); loader's hatch, with one door panel missing; and covers for the right and left loaders' periscopes. Lying toward the rear of the roof is the original cover for the rear hatch of the superstructure, with the interior side up.

The large, conical-headed bolts on the hull and superstructure passed through angled brackets on the interior of the vehicle, thus holding the superstructure to the hull. The reinforcing plates, the left one of which appears at the bottom left of the photo, helped secure the front corner of the superstructure to the hull.

On the deck to the front of the superstructure are the driver's hatch door, with three periscopes; the radio operator's hatch door; the air-intake grille for the two Maybach type HL 120 TRM engines, which were located to the rear of the driver's and radio operator's compartment; and, flanking the engine air intake, the radiator-fan exhaust louvers.

Between the louvers and the superstructure are three hinged access plates for the engine compartment. On the right-front side of the radio operator's hatch is the radio antenna mount, surrounded by a splash guard. Lifting eyes are fitted to the front corners of the engine compartment cover. Details of the gun shield are visible.

On the angled side plate to the rear of the left headlight is the driver's side vision slit. Three periscopes on the driver's hatch door provided him with forward vision. The two strips on the left fender were brackets for storing spare track links. Secured to the glacis next to the left headlight is a wooden jack block.

Part of the right radiator-fan exhaust louver is at the lower center. Situated at the rear of the deck to the front of the superstructure are hinged hoods that provided access to the engine compartment. *Vladimir Yakubov*

The round cover next to the engine-air intake grille on the deck in front of the superstructure allowed access to a valve in the engine compartment. A similar cover is visible on the other side of the grille. *Vladimir Yakubov*

The radio operator's hatch door is viewed from the right side of the vehicle, showing the two rear-mounted hinges. At the bottom is part of the radio antenna mount and surrounding splash guard. *Vladimir Yakubov*

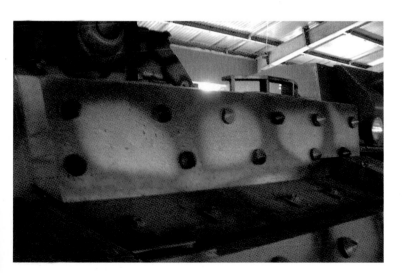

The front plate of the driver's and radio operator's compartment was formed from two plates of armor, each of which was 100 mm thick, bolted together to form a total thickness of 200 mm. *Vladimir Yakubov*

The front plate of the hull also was formed of two 100 mm plates of armor. The outer was cut to fit around the original towing attachments of the VK4501(P) but were replaced by adjacent towing eyes. *Vladimir Yakubov*

Much of the left suspension of the Ferdinand preserved at Kubinka is displayed. The hub of the idler was attached to its bearing with six conical-headed bolts, while the hub of the drive sprocket had twelve. *Vladimir Yakubov*

The left rear of the superstructure and upper hull of the Kubinka Ferdinand is displayed. A vertical welded seam is present on the hull above the bend in the fender accommodating the sprocket. *Vladimir Yakubov*

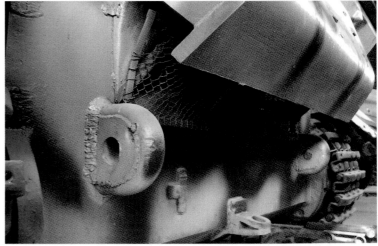

The left rear corner of the hull and superstructure is viewed close-up, showing the blackout taillight bracket and light guard and, to the lower right, part of the exhaust shroud for the electric motors. *Vladimir Yakubov*

The underside of the hot-air exhaust shroud for the electric motors is viewed. The screen was fitted to the opening of the shroud to prevent the enemy from tossing grenades or explosives into it. *Vladimir Yakubov*

The pistol-port plug on the right side of the superstructure is in view. The dovetailed joint of the side plate of the superstructure and the 80 mm thick rear plate of the superstructure is visible to the left. *Vladimir Yakubov*

The right rear of the superstructure and upper hull are observed. The bottom edge of the 80 mm thick side plates of the superstructure jutted out slightly from the top edge of the upper-hull side plate. *Vladimir Yakubov*

The roof of the superstructure is viewed facing the rear, with the commander's hatch to the left and the cover for the rear hatch of the superstructure to the rear. The edge of the cover was beveled. *Vladimir Yakubov*

CHAPTER 2
The Elefant Arrives

Elefant Fgst. Nr. (chassis number) 150040 of the 1st Platoon, 1st Company, schwere Panzerjäger-Abteilung 653, appears in markings and camouflage during the time the vehicle was assigned to the headquarters of Kampfgruppe Ulbricht, commanded by Lt. Helmut Ulbricht. American forces captured this Elefant after it was disabled and its crew abandoned it. Later, the vehicle was added to the collections of the US Army Ordnance Museum.

Following heavy Ferdinand losses during the Kursk offensive and its aftermath, the remaining vehicles were withdrawn to the Nibelungenwerke plant in Austria, where they were repaired and modernized beginning in January 1944.

One survey of the Kursk battlefield reported twenty-one Ferdinands littering the field, with most of the disabled vehicles located in the minefield. Soviet antitank mines, some made from large-caliber artillery rounds or aerial bombs, had damaged the track or suspension of more than half the vehicles. As a result, the immobilized Ferdinands were vulnerable to artillery strikes and roving antitank squads. As previously described, the Ferdinands were essentially defenseless against infantry attacks, and despite battlefield improvisations to fire a machine gun down the 88 mm gun barrel, it was clear that close-defense weapons needed to be added.

On the basis of the lessons learned in combat, a 7.92 mm MG 34 in a ball mount and fired by the radio operator was added at the hull front. The side vision slits for the radio operator and driver were sealed, and a visor was added to the driver's periscope. The commander's hatch was replaced with a cupola (similar to that found on the Sturmgeschütz III Ausf. G), providing a greater field of vision when the vehicle was "buttoned up."

Zimmerit, an antimagnetic-mine paste, was added to the vehicle, extending up to a height to cover the reach of an average man standing on the ground. Less obvious changes were also made, including relocating many items on the exterior of the vehicle. The mantlet shield was reversed, and the handles on the rear of the fighting compartment were removed to prevent aggressive Soviet antitank teams from climbing on the vehicle. These modifications increased the Ferdinand's weight from 65 to 70 tons.

The vehicle's name change came during the Ferdinand refit program, but it was not related to the process. The new name,

"Elefant," had been proposed in November 1943, and in February 1944 the change became official.

Following the rebuilding of the Ferdinand into the Elefant (German plural: Elefanten), the remanufactured vehicles were issued exclusively to schwere Panzerjäger-Abteilung 653 (s.Pz.Jäg. Abt. 653, or Heavy Tank Destroyer Battalion 653). On February 1, 1944, it was decided to dispatch the unit to Italy in an effort to stymie the Allied advance from the Anzio-Nettuno area. On February 11, the First Company of s.Pz.Jäg.Abt. 653 was re-formed with the Elefant, utilizing all eleven of the vehicles that had been completed as of that date. The troops and their vehicles arrived in Rome by train on February 24. By March 1, the unit had been thrust into combat and would remain there into July, when the unit was ordered home and three surviving Elefanten were sent to the Vienna Arsenal for rebuild. The combat capabilities of the Elefant in Italy were somewhat hampered by the vehicles' massive 70-ton weight, which was largely incompatible both with the road system and terrain in the country. This difficulty was compounded by an acute shortage of spare parts for the somewhat orphan design.

Rather than join the First Company in Italy, the Second and Third Companies of s.Pz.Jäg.Abt. 653 were returned to the Eastern Front in April, taking with them their newly remanufactured Elefanten. As with the Ferdinand, each company was equipped with fourteen vehicles, and the headquarters company was equipped with six Elefanten. As a result of attrition, by the time September 1944 arrived the number of Elefanten remaining stood at thirteen (or fourteen according to some sources). By the following month, s.Pz.Jäg.Abt. 653 was ordered to convert to the Jagdtiger, and all the surviving Elefanten were transferred to the newly formed schwere Panzerjäger Kompanie 614 (Heavy Tank Destroyer Company 614). This unit, which was created on December 15 from the Second Company of s.Pz.Jäg.Abt. 653, had thirteen or fourteen of the vehicles (sources differ). The unit remained on the Eastern Front until early 1945.

The final combat use of the Elefant was in the Königs Wusterhausen, Zossen, and Berlin areas near the end of the war. They were attached to Kampfgruppe "Ritter" (Combat Group "Ritter"), and evidence suggests that four of the Elefanten were employed in this defensive action. Reportedly, the absolute final action ended in the capture, by Soviet troops, of the last two examples of the Elefant on Karl-August-Platz and in the ruined Dreifaltigkeitskirche (Trinity Church) area of Berlin on May 1, 1945.

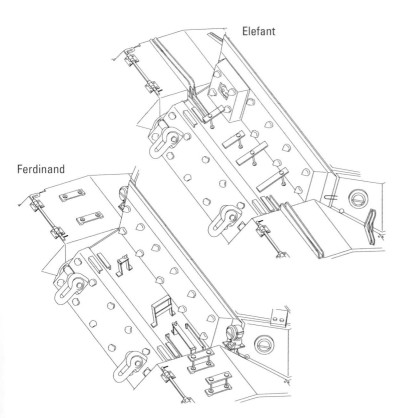

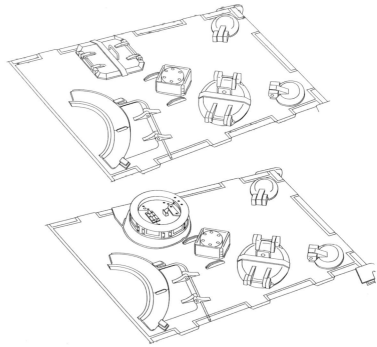

The rebuilding and subsequent renaming of the vehicles involved the addition of a bow machine gun. To install the weapon, a hole was torched in the front plate, forward of the radio operator. A thick armor piece with a ball mount was fixed over the hole, allowing installation of a 7.92 mm MG42 machine gun, which the radio operator would fire.

During the January–February 1944 rebuild, the flat commander's hatches of the Ferdinand (*left*) were replaced with a cupola similar to that used on the StuG III Ausf. G. At about the same time, the vehicles were renamed Elefant. The cupola-equipped superstructure is shown in the lower drawing.

Elefant number 102 of the 1st Company, schwere Panzerjäger-Abteilung 653, now at the US Army Ordnance Museum, displays its appearance after an early repainting effort following its capture. There is fresh paint where much of the Zimmerit had flaked off on the front of the hull. The gouges on the mantlet and gun are still there. *The Tank Museum*

After its capture, Elefant number 102 was scrutinized and tested by US Army Intelligence and Ordnance personnel. At this point, most of the vehicle's Zimmerit was intact. Several gouges from projectile strikes are visible on the gun shield and the front of the superstructure. The left fender was badly crumpled. *Military History Institute*

The letter *U* on the rear of the superstructure (for Kampfgruppe Ulbricht) and the number 102 were German markings; the rest of the markings were notices applied by the American captors. Even the lid of the tool box mounted on the hot-air outlet shroud at the rear of the hull has a coating of Zimmerit. The *Tank Museum*

In this photo, the lid has been removed from the tool box on Elefant number 102. The Zimmerit extended only partway up the sides and rear of the superstructure: just as high as an enemy soldier of average height could reach, since Zimmerit was intended to repel magnetic antitank mines stuck onto the vehicle by infantrymen. *Patton Museum*

US Army personnel, including one poking his head into the driver's hatch, inspect the captured "102" Elefant, presumably at the site in Italy where they found it. The irregular top limit of the Zimmerit on the side of the superstructure is apparent from this angle. Lying on top of the front of the fender is a towing clevis. *Patton Museum*

The "102" on the US-captured Elefant was over the central group of bolts holding the superstructure to the hull. The driver's and radio operator / front gunner's side vision slits were filled in on the Elefanten. Thus, when the front gunner was buttoned up in his compartment, his only view of the outside was through his gunsight. *Patton Museum*

Elefant 102 soon after its arrival at Aberdeen Proving Grounds. The Zimmerit antimagnetic application can still be seen. *Tom Laemlein collection*

Zimmerit was applied by hand with serrated trowels at the factory, and the patterns varied from vehicle to vehicle. Artistic is the only word for the patterns on the vertical plate in front of the driver's and bow gunner's compartment on Elefant number 102, with the radiating lines around the conical-headed bolts. *The Tank Museum*

Troopers of the Hermann Göring Division march past the disabled Elefant of Unteroffizier Werner Kühl of the 1st Company, schwere Panzerjäger-Abteilung 653. The tow cables are linked with small clevises to the larger clevises on the towing eyes: more convenient than removing the large clevises to attach the cables. *Thomas Anderson collection*

GIs survey the wreck of the Elefant commanded by Unteroffizier Werner Kühl of the 1st Company, schwere Panzerjäger-Abteilung 653. The vehicle was disabled in the Pontine Marshes near Anzio on February 28, 1944. The jack and tow cable on the ground are mementos of the Germans' failed efforts to recover the vehicle. *Patton Museum*

On February 29, 1944, one day after the loss of Kühl's Elefant, the 1/653 lost another Elefant, commanded by Oberfeldwebel Gustav Koss, in the Pontine Marshes. A mine blew off the front right road wheel. Although the crew repaired the track, recovery efforts failed, and the Germans detonated a charge in the vehicle to render it useless. *Patton Museum*

Koss's Elefant was photographed from the left side after it was disabled. Among its noteworthy features are the tow cable connected to a clevis on the right towing eye, the bent left mud flap, and the by-now-withered local camouflage that had been applied to the side of the vehicle. The front machine gun was still in place. *Patton Museum*

A bomb blast in an Italian town blew this Elefant of the 1st Company, schwere Panzerjäger-Abteilung 653, on its side, presenting a rare view of the superstructure roof. To the left are the loader's periscope covers and hatch, while to the right are the commander's cupola and gunner's periscope sliding and hinged covers. *The Tank Museum*

The same Elefant in the preceding photograph also was photographed from the front. The rear of the vehicle is to the right, with the underside of the hot-air exhaust shroud in view. Several access panels were on the bottom of the hull. Most of the road assemblies were blown off, but the left rear torsion-bar casing (*top*) is visible. *The Tank Museum*

This Elefant of the 1st Company, schwere Panzerjäger-Abteilung 653, served in Italy in 1944. The tactical number 102 is faintly visible on the side of the superstructure. The Gothic letter U on the rear of the superstructure signifies that it belonged to Kampfgruppe Ulbricht. The vehicle is now at the US Army Ordnance Museum. *The Tank Museum*

A still frame from a German film on the battles near Anzio/Nettuno in early 1944 depicts an Elefant rolling along an Italian road. *Tom Laemlein collection*

Elefant crew posed with their vehicle. The distinctive pattern of the Zimmerit antimagnetic paste is apparent. No MG 34 is in the socket mount. *Tom Laemlein collection*

After this Elefant of the 1st Company, schwere Panzerjäger-Abteilung 653, was disabled (its rear road assembly is missing), a recovery attempt was aborted and the crew tried to explode the vehicle in Soriano al Cimino, Italy. The detonation blew open the deck to the front of the superstructure. *The Tank Museum*

The same Elefant seen in the preceding photograph also was photographed from the front. Lying on the glacis is the torsion-bar casing from the right-rear road assembly. The left track was severed in several places, with part of the top run lying on top of the road wheels and the bottom run remaining in place below the wheels. Most of the left fender was missing. *The Tank Museum*

The crew of the Elefant abandoned in Soriano al Cimino probably had stowed the detached torsion-bar casing on the glacis with the intention of repairing the suspension when the vehicle reached a repair depot. It's not clear if the front deck over the engine and driver's and bow gunner's compartments would have been repairable. *The Tank Museum*

Curious citizens gather to look over Elefant number 124 of schwere Panzerjäger-Abteilung 653, abandoned in the piazza at Soriano al Cimino. In addition to the buckled front deck, the internal explosion also blew open the left engine compartment access door, exposing the rectangular ventilation opening on its interior side. One of the vehicle's road units is lying on the deck to the front of the driver's compartment. *Patton Museum*

A wrecker with a 6-ton Bilstein crane is backed up to an Elefant, preparing to do repairs on the tank destroyer. Lying on the ground next to the Elefant is a sprocket assembly. The entire superstructure roof is covered with a tarpaulin. Next to the Ferdinand is an SdKfz 251 half-track. *Thomas Anderson collection*

The crew of Elefant 332 is stowing the 16-pound 88 × 822 mm R armor-piercing shells for the 8.8 cm Pak 43/2 L/71 main gun. The height of the Zimmerit application is apparent. *Tom Laemlein collection*

A repair crew is using a flatbed wrecker truck with a Bilstein 6-ton crane to either lift or lower the deck of an Elefant. This operation was necessary when replacing or performing major maintenance on the engines and generators. Note the brave crewman inside the vehicle underneath the raised deck. *Thomas Anderson collection*

The removed deck hovers over the forward compartments of an Elefant during major maintenance operations, probably involving the engines and generators. Leaning against the front of the superstructure is the raised right engine compartment cover, revealing its dark paint tone, possibly red primer or dark-gray paint. *Thomas Anderson collection*

Crewmen lounge around a battle-scarred Elefant. The muzzle brake of the 88 has been shot away from the rear baffle forward. In the position where the driver's sealed-up vision slit was located, there appears to be a gaping hole, either from a direct hit or from the removal of the round plate incorporating the slit. *Thomas Anderson collection*

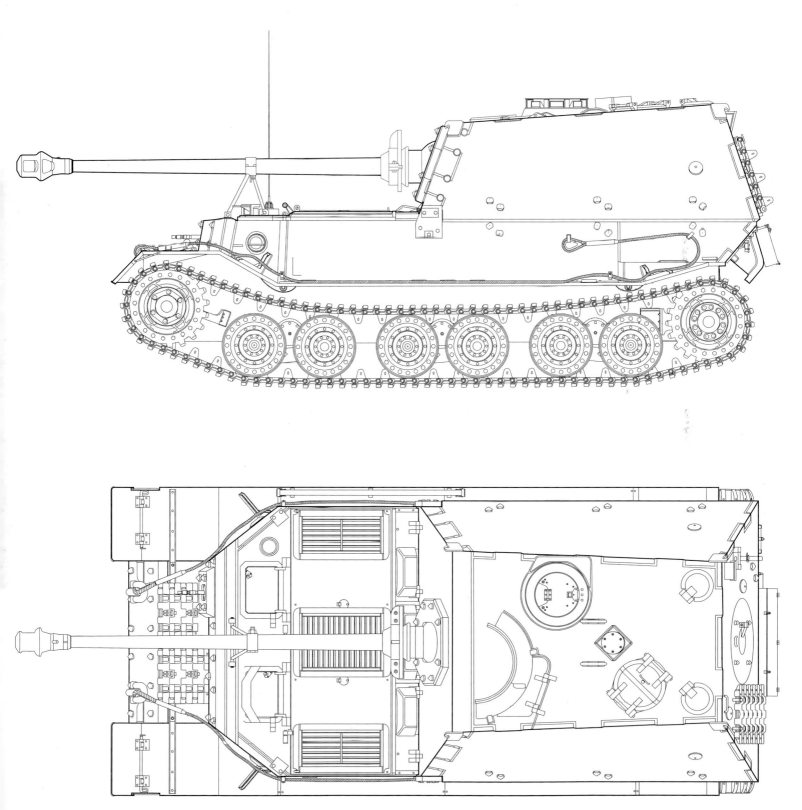

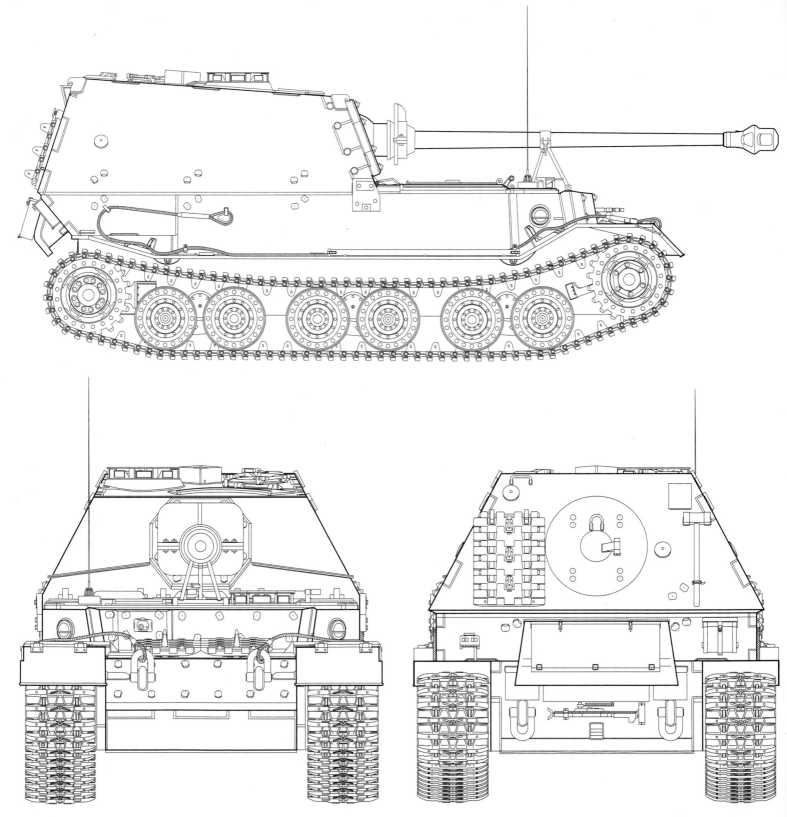

The Elefant tank destroyers were reworked versions of existing Ferdinand tank destroyers that received factory upgrades at Porsche's Nibelungenwerke and the Vienna Arsenal from late January to early April 1944. Several exterior details were changed, such as the addition of a machine gun ball mount to the front of the radio operator's compartment and the replacement of the Kgs 62/600/130 tracks with wider Kgs 64/640/130 tracks.

During their factory upgrades, Elefanten were given a coat of Zimmerit paste, a textured cement intended to repel magnetic mines, on vertical surfaces of the hull and the lower part of the superstructure. The Zimmerit was removed from the US Army Ordnance Museum's Elefant at some point after its capture. The paint job is recent, and the camouflage scheme is not identical to the original one.

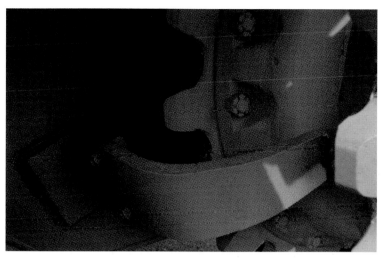

The Elefant's idler assemblies had two sets of sprockets, each with nineteen teeth. The idler hubs were secured to the bearings with six conical-headed bolts. The sprockets were fastened to each spoke with two hex bolts and locking nuts.

A scraper bolted to an L-shaped bracket welded to the hull acted to keep mud from building up between the idler hub and the track. The solid inner rim of the idler was attached to the sprockets with locking nuts and bolts.

The right-front road wheel is shown in close-up. The heads of the hex bolts that held the rim to the hub and those that secured the hubcap were prevented from working loose by locking tabs, with one side bent up against a facet of the head.

A rubber ring bushing within each bogie-wheel assembly served as a cushion between the steel tires and the bogie wheels. The rubber of the bushings is visible through the holes around the outer perimeter of the wheels.

The hub of the drive sprocket (*left*) was fastened to its bearing with twelve conical-headed bolts, eight of which are secured with locking strips, two bolts per strip. Note that the four-spoked outer wheel of the drive sprocket varies in design from that of the idler. Between the sprocket and the rear road wheel, part of the rear mud scraper is visible.

A more complete view of the right-rear mud scraper and its mounting bracket is visible from this angle. Closer details are provided of several of the locking strips for the hub bolts on the drive sprocket. The inner rim of the drive sprocket assembly is solid, rather than spoked. At the top, several track guides are in view.

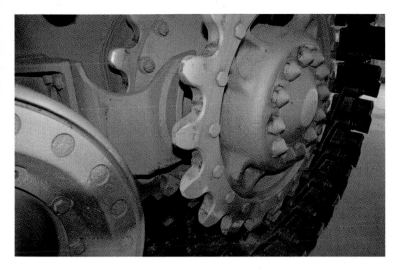

The mud scraper is visible between the bogie wheel (*left*) and the left drive sprocket. Through the holes in the rim of the bogie wheel, the rubber ring bushing that served as a cushion for the wheel and its tire is visible.

The underside of the left fender where it angles upward to the side of the driver's compartment is viewed. Toward the right are two steel skids that protected the bottom of the fender from rubbing and damage by the track.

A bogie wheel is viewed from above. These wheels were an adaptation of Soviet-type, cushioned-tire bogie wheels. They were fabricated from pressed sheet metal with rubber-cushioned steel tires and were 31.26 inches in diameter.

The Ferdinand and Tiger (P) suspension included three bogie units per side, with a cylindrical torsion-bar housing mounted at the bottom of each bogie unit. The forward left bogie unit is viewed from beneath the front of the vehicle.

From the right rear, and shorn of its Zimmerit, the Elefant looks little different than the Ferdinand, with the exception of the commander's cupola protruding above the roof and the absence of the tool box on the side of the hull toward the front. On the Elefant, the tool box was relocated to the hot-air exhaust shroud on the rear of the hull, but the box is missing on this example.

The three steel ladder rungs welded to the left side of the superstructure of the Ferdinands were cut off as part of the Elefant modification, since the ladders would have interfered with the stowage of the spare track links. The short, vertical steel rods welded to the left side of the superstructure are vestiges of the ladders.

Details of the rear hatch cover are provided in this close-up. The small port in the center was meant for ejecting the spent 88 mm casings but could as easily be used for passing ammunition into the fighting compartment. The U-shaped rod welded above the port was a lifting eye for removing the cover with a hoist.

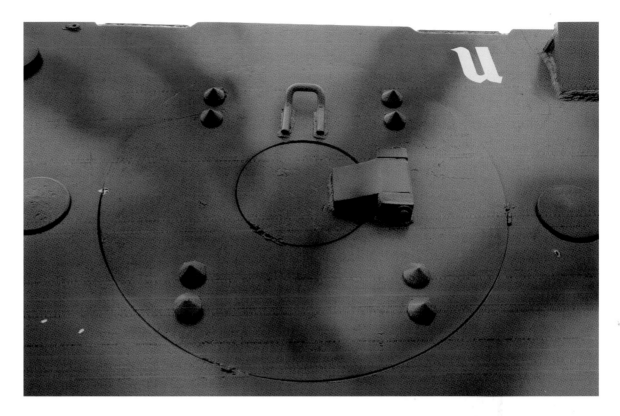

The pistol-port plugs flanking the hatch cover are replacements. The original plugs presented a conical appearance on their exterior side. To the right side are, *top to bottom*, the right-rear lifting hook, command antenna mount, bracket for the sledgehammer head, and clamp bracket for the sledgehammer handle. The hatch cover has been tack-welded shut.

The left spare-track hook was present when this vehicle was captured by the Americans in 1944 but has since been broken off, leaving only a trace of the part. Flanking the right spare-track hook are the remnants of the center ladder rung. At the top center is the upper rear pistol port, with what appears to be its original steel plug.

Below the hot-air exhaust at the lower center of the hull is the towing pintle. The purpose of the curved pieces of sheet steel welded to the hull above the towing eyes is unclear. Remnants of the blackout taillight bracket and the conduit for the light's power cable are above the track.

The hot-air exhaust shroud, seen from the right side, was fabricated from welded armor plate. The diamond-tread plate to the right is the rear of the right fender. Above the fender, details of the dovetail joint between the side and rear armored plates of the hull are visible.

Cast from manganese steel, the Kgs 64/640/130 tracks are 640 mm (25.2 inches) wide and have a pitch of 130 mm (5.12 inches). Part of the Elefant modifications was the relocation of the jack from the glacis in front of the driver's compartment to the rear of the lower hull, and remnants of the jack brackets are in evidence.

In this view upward from the lower rear of the Elefant, the hot-air outlet on the underside of the shroud is visible. This example lacks the wire screen usually installed to prevent enemy infantry from tossing grenades into the outlet. At the lower center is the towing pintle.

The left side of Elefant no. 102, Fgst. Nr. 150071, at the US Army Ordnance Museum shows several modifications made during the early 1944 upgrades, including reinforced radiator air grilles on the deck to the front of the superstructure, and the gun shield installed with the mounting flanges and bolts toward the front.

At the rear of each side of the upper hull of the Ferdinand and Elefant, just below the superstructure, a rectangular plate was welded on to extend the hull aft in a straight line because the sides of the upper hull tapered inward at this point; this was a vestige of the design of the Ferdinand's ancestor, the VK4501(P). This tapering is visible in the space below that plate.

The outside edge of the fender was bent down to give it additional strength. During the 1944 modifications program, four supports were added to the tops of the fenders, one at each former of the upper hull. The supports within the triangular recesses at the rear of the hull are missing from this example, but a mounting block is faintly visible.

A reinforcing plate is bolted to the superstructure and hull on both sides at the lower front corners of the superstructure. On the front of the superstructure at the top of the photo is the left rain gutter, an improvement standardized in the Elefant upgrades in 1944, intended to keep water from running down into the engine compartment.

Running across the deck immediately to the front of the superstructure are three hinged covers to provide access to the engine compartment and cooling-water fillers. Above the covers is the left rain gutter, and to the upper left is the left side of the gun shield. A gouge from a projectile hit above the top of the gutter has been painted silver for emphasis.

A projectile hit is marked in silver near the bottom front edge of the side-hull extension, next to the left-hand idler. Three other large hits are picked out in silver on the front of the superstructure and to the left of the gun mount next to the shield. Numerous other small gouges are marked in silver as well.

Welded to the upper front plate at the front of the hull are two towing eyes. The mud flaps to the front of both fenders were hinged for ease of accessing and cleaning the area over the idlers.

The gouge from a projectile hit on the lower front edge of the hull side plate is visible next to the track. The side plates of the lower hull were 80 mm thick. An extra 30 mm plate was welded to the bottom of the Elefant's hull below the driver's and radio operator's compartment for added protection against mines.

Coil springs were fitted to the outer sides of the mud flaps to help keep them in place. In addition to the fender supports at the four corners of the upper hull, introduced with the Elefant improvements, new supports were added toward the front of each fender. These were made of steel channels.

The side vision slits of the Elefanten were welded shut. Below and to the rear of the disk that formerly contained the right vision slit, the top of one of the fender supports introduced with the Elefant is visible. The overall thickness of the two-ply armor to the front of the driver's compartment is apparent.

The 100 mm thick plate bolted to the upper facet of the front of the hull was cut out on both sides to fit around the towing attachments that were part of the VK4501(P) but were not removed when those chassis were converted to Ferdinand/Elefant tank destroyers and new towing eyes were incorporated.

Several links of spare track, painted black, are stowed on the glacis of this Elefant. Although spare-track brackets were added to the left rear of the superstructure of Elefanten, crews sometimes continued to stash spare tracks on the fronts of the vehicles, sometimes positioning them to offer increased protection from enemy projectiles.

The 100 mm armor plate fitted over the Kugelblende 100 ball mount has beveled edges and is attached with four conical-headed bolts. The right edge of the plate was shaped to accommodate two of the bolts on the 100 mm frontal plate. Note how, even though that frontal plate is bolted in place, its edge is also welded to the 100 mm plate behind it.

The rough rectangular pattern to the right of the disk that formerly incorporated the radio operator's vision slit is where the original Ferdinand headlight bracket was removed; the circular pattern below it is the filled-in hole for the light cable. The fender supports added during the Elefant upgrades were fabricated from welded and gusseted channels. This one, toward the bottom center of the photo on the front right of the hull, is welded to the hull and bolted to the fender.

As seen from above, the front support bracket of the left fender is to the left of the spare track links. The pattern of the diamond tread of the fender is displayed. Also, the top edges of the frontal armor of the driver's and radio operator's compartment are visible at the bottom.

The right front of the Elefant is viewed from atop the radio operator / bow gunner's position. A fine welding bead is visible between the top of the 100 mm armor plate of the bow machine gun and the 100 mm frontal armor behind it. Remnants of weld beads, evidently representing removed hardware, are visible on the glacis.

Tracks are shown close-up. Originally, the Kgs 62/600/130 tracks were installed on the Ferdinands. These were 600 mm wide, with a 130 mm pitch, and were of a single-pin, single-guide, dry-bearing design. During the 1944 modernization program, the Elefanten were given the Kgs 64/640/130 tracks, with a width of 640 mm and pitch of 130 mm.

The deck from the engine access covers in front of the superstructure to the front of the driver's / bow gunner's compartment was of one section and could be removed for maintenance and replacement of the generators and engine. One of the lifting eyes for the deck is in the foreground, on the front corner of the right radiator air grille.

Supporting the 88 mm gun barrel is a collapsible tripod travel lock with a brace to the rear. On top of the lock is a clamp with a large wing-nut tightener. To the lower right is the mount for the driver's three periscopes.

The travel lock is viewed from the right side. The radio operator's / bow gunner's hatch door is to the lower left. One of the Elefant improvements was the addition of the sunshade extending from the top front of the driver's periscope housing.

The right side of the yoke of the travel lock and its clamping bolt and wing nut are viewed from a different angle. The tops of the two front legs of the travel lock are welded to the bottom of the yoke, while the top of the rear brace is hinged to the yoke with a bolt.

The three new, raised louvers added over the original locations of the air intake vents on the deck are visible. These louvers were part of the Elefant modifications in early 1944 and were designed to increase the intakes' protection from splinters. The two outer louvers, over the radiators, have a grab handle on each side.

The center and right engine access covers are replacements, lacking the ventilator hoods and openings of the original parts. The cover on the left side of the vehicle appears to be original, with the ventilator hood intact. The diagonal weld line along the front of the superstructure marks where the gutter was torn off.

The housing for the driver's three periscopes on his hatch door is viewed from the center front of the Elefant. Welded to the top of the housing is the sunshade. Above the far side of the periscope housing is the hold-open latch for the driver's door.

Details of the front deck of the Elefant are illustrated, including, to the right, the right-front leg and rear brace of the travel lock. To hold the radio operator's hatch door open, the latch with the knurled grip at the center of the photo engaged with the bent piece of metal projecting from the side of the door.

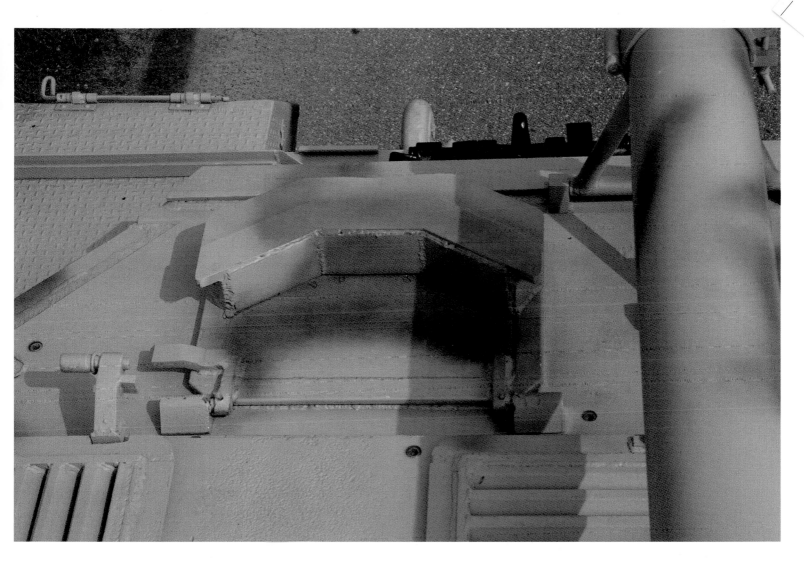

A view of the periscope housing from behind reveals that its back was fabricated from three rectangular plates welded together. On top of the housing are two separate pieces: the original top of the housing and the sunshade extending to the front.

When the driver's hatch door was locked in the open position, pulling the knurled handle on the hold-open latch released it so it could be closed. There is a bullet hole in the side of the housing. The view is from the left side of the 88 mm gun while facing forward.

The radiator and engine air intakes were fabricated from welded parts. The hole provided access to a valve in the engine/generator compartment; there was a similar hole on the other side of the grille to the right, and both holes now lack their hinged covers.

The front edge of the radio operator's hatch on the Ordnance Museum's Elefant is bent and chipped. Visible under the door is a raised coaming, welded around the hatch opening, designed to keep water on the deck from spilling into the compartment.

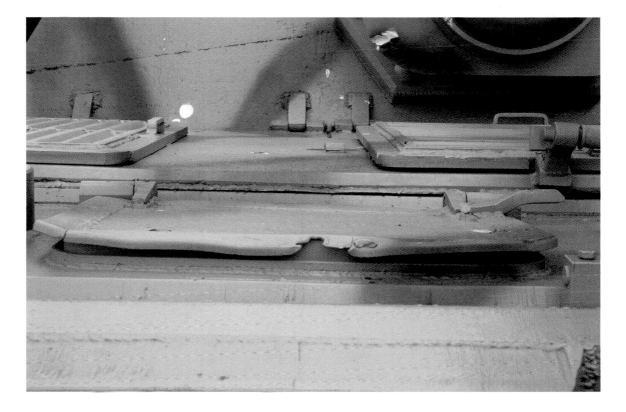

At the base of the splash guard for the antenna mount to the left is a small hole through the weld joint to allow water to flow out. Hatch-door hold-open latches are visible at the upper center and in the background above the driver's periscope housing.

At the base of the splash guard for the antenna mount to the left is a small hole through the weld joint to allow water to flow out. Hatch-door hold-open latches are visible at the upper center and in the background above the driver's periscope housing.

From the left side, details of the driver's periscope housing and hold-open latch are visible. A triangular gusset was roughly welded to the sunshade and the side of the periscope housing to support the sunshade.

The left side of the travel lock is displayed from behind. The object with the two C-shaped hooks between the two hatches is the latch for the base of the rear brace of the travel lock. At the bottom of the brace are rotating, squared studs, part of the brace's locking mechanism.

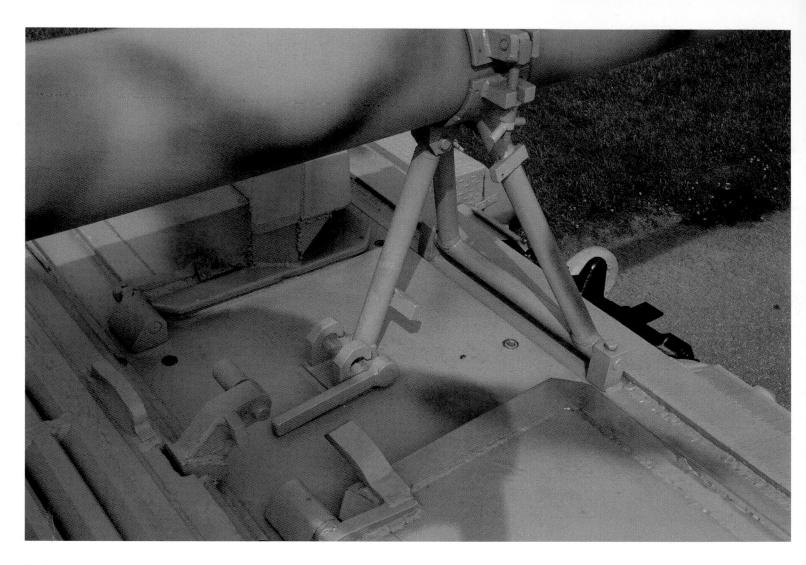

To lock the bottom of the rear brace of the travel lock, the rotating studs were inserted into the gaps in the front of the latch, and the locking handle to the right side of the brace was turned to lock the brace in place. A stop for the locking handle protrudes from the right leg of the travel lock.

A left-side view of the barrel of the 88 mm PaK 43/2 L/71 cannon shows the gouging on the shield incurred by a large-caliber projectile. The octagonal armor plate over the opening in the superstructure for the cannon is 100 mm thick.

The welded construction of the gun shield is evident in this photo. Two bolts through the horizontal flanges on each side of the gun barrel locked the two halves of the shield together.

The 88 mm gun had an elevation of +18° to −8° and a traverse of 15° to either side. The gun could reach maximum elevation only when aimed straight ahead. The ball on the gun mount provided protective cover for the gun aperture in the front of the superstructure.

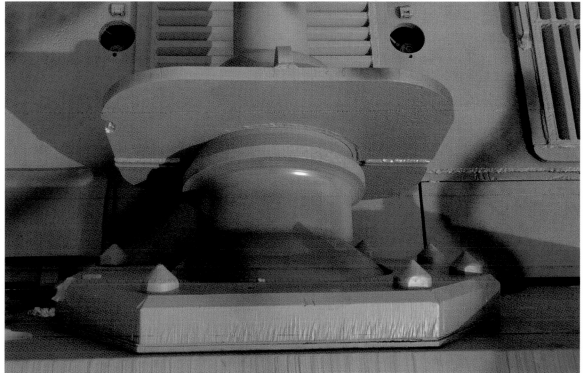

A downward view of the gun barrel, housing, and shield from the roof of the superstructure emphasizes the shape of the barrel housing and ball mount. The first Ferdinands lacked gun shields and were retrofitted with them in the field.

The Elefant's 88 mm PaK 43/2 L/71 was 21.94 feet long from the rear of the breech to the front of the muzzle brake, with a barrel length of 20.67 feet. The L/71 in the gun's designation meant the length of the barrel was seventy-one times the width of the bore.

The roof of the superstructure covered the fighting compartment of the Elefant. Prominent in the foreground are the gunner's periscope aperture and covers (*right*) and the commander's cupola. A result of the modification program of early 1944, the cupola replaced the square, flush, two-door hatch of the Ferdinand.

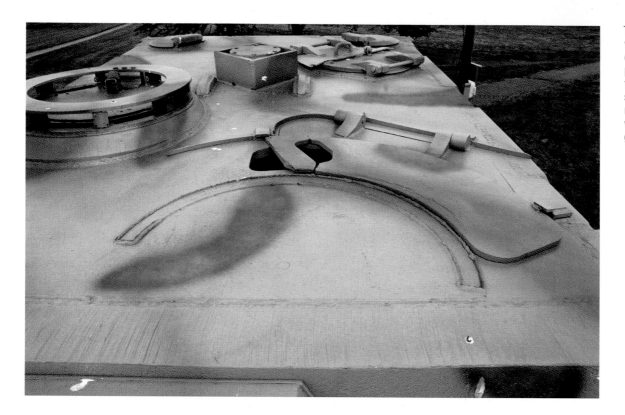

The gunner's Sfl.SF.1 periscope would have protruded through the oval opening at the center of the photo, between the two plates of the curved cover. The cover would slide in unison with the lateral movement of the periscope, which was linked to the movement of the gun.

The periscope cover slid within tracks and retainer brackets. To the rear of the sliding cover is a hinged cover that could be opened to accommodate the rearward movement of the periscope when the gun was brought to maximum elevation. Toward the bottom is the top edge of the 200 mm frontal plate of the superstructure.

The thickness of the gunner's periscope cover in the foreground is evident in this view from the left front of the superstructure. A side view is also provided of the commander's cupola, topped with an armored ring that served to protect the periscopes.

The semicircular weld lines to the front of the sliding cover of the gunner's periscope once secured in place the front track/retainer for that cover, now missing. In the background are the ventilator, loaders' and gunner's hatch, and, in the far corner of the superstructure roof, the left loader's periscope cover.

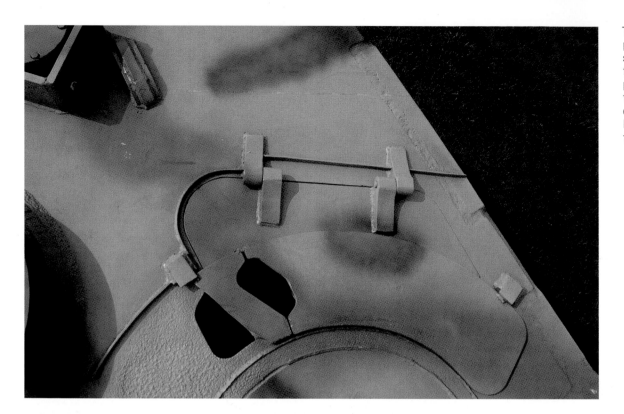

The sliding cover of gunner's periscope protected the crescent-shaped slot in the roof under it from enemy fire. The inboard piece of the cover (to the left in the photo) has been cut down considerably; originally it would have been of even greater length than the outboard piece.

To the rear of the sliding and hinged covers for the gunner's periscope are thin strips of steel welded to the turret roof. They served as rain gutters, preventing water from rolling down the sloping roof and into the periscope opening.

The commander's cupola included a two-piece hatch door and openings for seven periscopes around its perimeter. Next to the hatch door hinge is a door stop with a rubber bumper. At the rear corner of the roof is the cover for the right loader's periscope.

This photo illustrates the relative positions of the commander's cupola, ventilator, loaders' hatch, and loaders' periscope hatches and hinged covers. The interleaved joints between the superstructure's roof and side plates are visible along the edge of the roof.

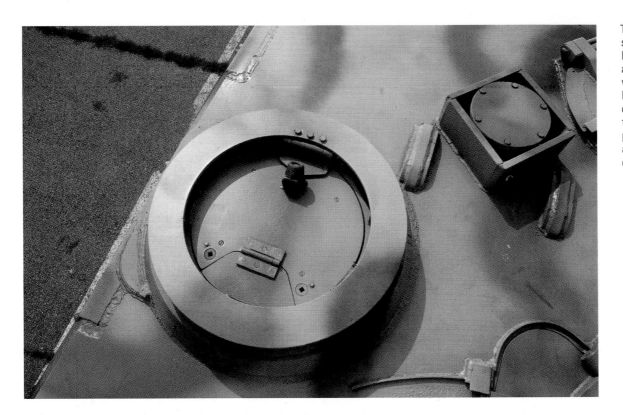

The commander could open the small, hinged panel at the front of his hatch door, in order to extend an SF.14Z scissors periscope without having to open the whole hatch and expose himself to enemy fire. On the main panel of the door to each side of the small panel is a hex socket that accepted a key for unlocking the door from the outside.

The remnant of one periscope mount is still in place on the commander's cupola. Because of the downward slope of the superstructure roof toward the front, the front of the cupola's base is thicker than the rear of the base.

The fighting compartment ventilator is enclosed by a protective enclosure fabricated from welded armor, and on it a gouge from a projectile is painted silver. The two objects welded to the roof next to the ventilator are external extensions of the brackets for an interior travel lock over the breech of the 88 mm gun.

In view from the commander's cupola (*lower left*) toward the left rear corner of the superstructure roof are the ventilator, loaders' and gunner's hatch, and left loader's periscope cover. Note the heavy weld beads at the vertical corners of the ventilator splash guard.

An overhead view shows the Elefant's commander's cupola (*lower left*), ventilator and tightly fitting splash guard, and loaders' and gunner's hatch. The latter hatch, with its raised base and two doors forming a circle, remained unchanged from the Ferdinand.

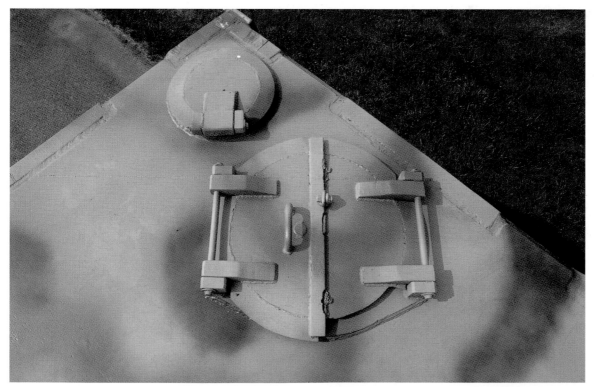

Both loaders' and gunner's hatch doors were secured to the hinges on the base of the hatch with long, exposed hinge pins. A grab handle is on the rear door. The hinged cover at the roof's rear corner protected an opening for a periscope, operated by a loader.

A low-angle view shows further details of the construction of the hatch and its doors. A thin steel strip covered the gap between the doors when closed. The exterior extensions to the interior travel lock brackets (one is shown to the left) were necessary to strengthen the apparatus, given the thin (30 mm) roof armor.

Viewed from the side, the cover for the left loader's periscope has a low profile and beveled edges. The hinge is welded to the top of the cover. A clear view is provided of part of the welded, interleaved joint between the roof and the left side of the superstructure.

A low-angle view from the commander's cupola facing the rear shows the right loader's periscope cover and the interleaved joint between the roof and the right side of the superstructure. At the bottom center is the rubber bumper of the cupola hatch door.

A downward view of the right loader's periscope cover reveals that it was fabricated by welding a beveled outer ring to a round central piece. The loaders' periscopes were an essential part of the crew's ability to monitor the vehicle's surroundings during combat.

In 2017, the Elefant traveled to England to take part in a special exhibition at the Tank Museum, Bovington Camp, dubbed *The Tiger Collection*, during which this and the following photo were taken. This was the first time that the vehicle had left the United States since World War II. *Massimo Foti*

The last-recorded combat of the Elefant occurred on April 22, 1945, when four of the vehicles assigned to schwere Panzerjäger-Kompanie 614 supported Battle Group Ritter in the defense of Zossen, near Berlin. With that action, the Elefant concluded a service career that had begun with the delivery of the Ferdinand two years earlier. *Massimo Foti*

The Tiger Collection exhibition lasted for two years, after which the only surviving Elefant was returned to indoor storage at Fort Lee, Virginia, United States. The Ferdinand/Elefant had proved to be a mixed blessing; it was a proven tank killer, racking up an impressive record against Allied armor. Its armor was proof against all but the most-powerful antitank weapons. It also was not without its faults, having rather fragile tracks; trouble-prone engines, cooling systems, and dynamos; very limited visibility for the crew; and a gun that was prone to jamming, frequently requiring a hammer and chisel to extract jammed rounds. Better tank killers would supersede the Ferdinand/Elefant, but it remains a unique and impressive example of German tank-hunter design and thinking. *Author*

While no longer on public display, as it was when exposed to the elements at the Ordnance Museum at Aberdeen Proving Ground, the Elefant is now displayed indoors in the US Army Ordnance Training Support Facility at Fort Lee, Virginia, preserving it for future generations. Even though it is now surrounded by much more modern and powerful weapons, the famed tank hunter still looks quite formidable. *Author*